Spiritual Reflections Journal

Health Ministry Edition

Spiritual Reflections Journal
Health Ministry Edition

Dr. Sharon T. Hinton DMIN, RN-BC, MSN

PepTalk Productions
2015

First Printing: 2010

Second Printing: 2015

ISBN 978-0-9965930-0-7

PepTalk Productions
312 W. Georgia St.
Floydada, TX 79235

www.SharonTHinton.com

Ordering Information:

Special discounts are available on quantity purchases by corporations, associations, educators, and others. For details, contact the publisher at the above listed address.

U.S. trade bookstores and wholesalers: Please contact PepTalk Productions or email Sharon@SharonTHinton.com.

Contents

Introduction

We all need personal time alone with our Creator. Prayer, journaling, meditation, and solitude are examples of finding that time. This journal is a tool to assist you in your time alone with God to hear not only what God says to you, but also to hear what your inner-self is saying. Give the private words of your soul permission to speak so that you may respond as the Holy Spirit leads.

There are no rules of grammar here…spelling doesn't count, sentences need not be complete, and thoughts need not be in words. Doodles, colors, textures, pictures, poetry, music and anything else that speaks to you is appropriate. **No one** will be grading or even looking at your journal unless you choose to share.

God is present within the circumstances of your life and acts to deepen your awareness of the good and the holy. If you are to find deeper insights and inspirations, you must take time to reflect. It is a way of noticing more than the everyday surface of your life that connects your faith and traditions to your ministry. Journals enable you to move through the fog of your life to clarity: to see, feel and live in the light of your inner-self. Journals provide perspective to the past, reveal insight into the future, and make the present an opportunity for self-examination and understanding.

Note: While the activities in this workbook are based on Christian principles, they are applicable to all faiths. Should you have questions or concerns about your journal entries, feel free to share them with someone you trust to guide you spiritually.

It is time now to start your personal journey. Peace and joy be with you as you travel through this journal.

Dr. Sharon T. Hinton, DMIN, RN-BC, MSN

Day 1: Who Am I?

Spiritual growth does not refer to only one aspect of life. It concerns all of life – our goals, our time, our relationships, our work, our politics, our inner selves. This activity's goal is to become reacquainted with yourself and what you want. Writing is a good way to have time alone. Being alone isn't always easy because you come face-to-face with your strengths and your weaknesses, but it is the perfect time to come face-to-face with God.

Take a deep breath. Pray that your journaling time will be fruitful and that you may hear God as he speaks. Expect the Holy Spirit to lead you as you journal. Often when you review, you will wonder where the words came from because they are not yours. This is your affirmation that God is speaking through your writing.

You are more than the roles you play. Like an onion, you must peel away the layers and the masks you wear for others to find yourself. Close your eyes and think about yourself. Allow the images, metaphors, feelings, and thoughts to present themselves to you.

Now write, trying to stay focused inward. Do not evaluate or judge, just write, don't censor or try to interpret, just write. Don't be legalistic. Write exactly what comes to mind. SPELLING DOESN'T COUNT!

<u>WHO AM I?</u>

I am _____

_____

_____

I am _____

_____

_____

I am _____

_____

_____

I am _____

_____

_____

I am _____

_____

_____

I am _____

_____

_____

What do you find looking at your list? Below are sample categories with an example for each. You may have additional categories. Don't worry that you must fill each one.

Role: *(a nurse)*_____

_____

Body: *(short)*_____

_____

Personality: *(a people person)*_____

_____

Faith: *(Christian)*_____

_____

Talents: *(a pianist)*_____

_____

Metaphors: *(small fish in a big pond)*_____

_____

Colors: *(sunny yellow disposition)*_____

_____

Emotions: *(stressed)*_____

_____

Animals: *(like a tiger)*_____

_____

Other: _____

_____

Write for 3-5 minutes about what the last section revealed to you. No editing or judgments just observe what your writing reveals and use the insight as you need to.

_____

_____

_____

_____

_____

_____

_____

_____

_____

_____

_____

_____

_____

_____

_____

_____

_____

Journaling Tips

- If thoughts or worries keep interrupting your writing, turn to an empty page and start a list – there the interruptions are saved for later attention, quieting your mind so that you can concentrate.

- If you have a major worry, take ten minutes and write specifically about that worry – what it is – how it makes you feel – what might be done about it – write nonstop whatever comes into your mind without editing. This is a great technique to clear your mind of mental and emotional distractions so that you can hear the still quiet voice of God speaking to you. Journals are where you can think through life's problems with prayerful contemplation and find answers that might otherwise be lost. Journals are proof that God is in control.

Day 2: Examine Your Relationship with God

Anyone who seriously seeks God faces doubts from time to time. Where or who can you go to for answers? Asking questions is important, but defining your beliefs and finding a way to express your beliefs in your day to day life is also important. It is the "so-what?" factor. Today you will make some statements about faith, describe how you find acceptance and forgiveness, and express your doubts.

The word "write" is used 78 times in 69 verses of Christian scripture. (Stewart, *A Book of Life*) A journal is a great place for personal truth, for insight, and forgiveness. God meets you as you give words to the holy work in your life. This exercise asks you to take the time to think through and clarify what you believe. As you bring your beliefs into focus, you will have the courage to share with others.

Reflection:

> **1 Peter 3:15**
>
> *Always be prepared to give an answer to everyone who asks you to give the reason for the hope that you have.*

Think about these words: God, Jesus, Holy Spirit, Faith, Forgiveness, Grace, Child of God, Christian, Religion, Spirituality, Walk with God, Prayer, Salvation, Sin.[1]

After you answer the following questions, write some of your own.

● What do you think you are supposed to believe?

_____

_____

_____

_____

_____

_____

● Why do you believe what you do?

_____

_____

_____

_____

_____

_____

---

[1] *Note: If you are from a faith other than Christianity, substitute the appropriate terminology for your belief system.*

How do you know God exists?

_____

_____

_____

_____

_____

What does God have to do with you and your daily life?

_____

_____

_____

_____

_____

How does prayer work?

_____

_____

_____

_____

_____

Questions I would really like to have answered:

1. _____
   _____

2. _____
   _____

3. _____
   _____

4. _____
   _____

5. _____
   _____

People and places that I can go to for answers:

1. _____
   _____

2. _____
   _____

3. _____
   _____

4. _____
   _____

5. _____
   _____

Journaling Tips

- Everyone is busy and it is not always possible to carry a journal around, so use sticky notes or the notes feature on your phone as thoughts occur. Put them in your journal at the end of the day and rewrite them when you have time.

- Change colors of ink once in a while to change your perspective.

Day 3: What Do You Really Believe?

What do you believe? Have you ever thought about this seriously? Some people are "religious" their entire life and never take the time to look inside to examine their beliefs or why they believe what they believe. Write a statement of your belief. Don't worry about spelling or grammar. You don't even have to use complete sentences unless you want to. Don't give what you think others would expect you to say, be completely honest with yourself. Use your own words, not some religious cliché you have heard. Write only what you honestly believe for sure first.

What I Believe...

…about God:

_____

_____

…about Jesus:

_____

_____

…about the Holy Spirit:

_____

_____

…about church:

_____

_____

…about the Bible:

_____

_____

…about my faith walk:

_____

_____

…about my future:

_____

_____

…about having a life of faith:

_____

_____

…about faith community nursing/health ministry:

_____

_____

…God is calling me to do:

_____

_____

Now, write about your questions and doubts. (Yes, everyone has questions and doubts!)

_____

_____

_____

_____

_____

_____

_____

_____

What do you need or want to know more about?

_____

_____

_____

_____

_____

_____

_____

_____

_____

Reflection:

Being a person of faith means being willing to accept yourself with all the strengths and weaknesses. It means being able to be a whole person including the shadows and doubts. To accept others, we must first accept ourselves. Forgiveness of others and ourselves is a continuous process. Sometimes it is easier to forgive others than it is to forgive ourselves.

Think about a time that you forgave someone. Write about the experience. How did you feel? Was it hard to forgive?

_____

_____

_____

_____

_____

_____

_____

_____

_____

Think about a time that you forgave yourself. Write about the experience. How did you feel? Was it harder to forgive yourself or someone else?

_____

_____

_____

_____

_____

_____

_____

_____

Now the hard question! Do you keep bringing up past situations to yourself? Do you continue to punish yourself for mistakes that were supposedly forgiven? When God forgives, the page is erased and never brought up again. How does your way of forgiving compare to God's?

_____

_____

_____

_____

_____

_____

_____

_____

Journaling Tips

• If you are having trouble getting started try using an alpha poem to capture your thoughts. Choose a word and write using each letter as a starting point for a sentence. The words do not need to rhyme and you are free to use more than one word. Examples for the words journal and time:

Just a few letters on the page
Out of my heart and soul onto the paper
Under the surface are words of wisdom
Reaching out to myself
No other tool
Allows me to be me
Like my journal

Ticking
In
Minutes to
Eternity

Day 4: Why You Exist in This Place at This Point in Time

It is natural to wonder why you are here from time to time. We all have a need for purpose – we all want to know what our mission in this life is. God created you in this time and place for a reason. If you are not sure of God's plan for your life, creating a personal mission statement is a good place to start looking for answers. It is hard to move forward unless you have a direction to start toward.

A journal gives you a picture of where you have come from, where you are now, and where you seem to be heading. For the person of faith, it is important to become what God intended you to become. We all have a strong sense that our lives are supposed to matter, that we have a part to play in the unfolding story of God's kingdom. Who we become and what we do is important. The challenge is to find the future God has planned for your specific gifts and talents. In your journal, you are free to envision any desired future, clarify life purposes, establish goals, and explore ways to move toward your goals.

Write your personal mission statement.

_____

_____

_____

_____

_____

_____

_____

_____

_____

_____

Reflection:

> **Luke 6:37**
>
> *Judge not, and you will not be judged;*
> *condemn not, and you will not be condemned;*
> *forgive, and you will be forgiven.*

Pray for insight and faith. Review what you have written over the past few days. Clarify and add to your thoughts as needed with a different color of ink. What have you discovered about yourself? What are you doing or going to do differently to treat yourself more like a child of God instead of an orphan?

_____

_____

_____

_____

_____

_____

_____

_____

_____

_____

Look up Jeremiah 29:11 and Psalms 20:4. What are these scriptures saying to you?

_____

_____

_____

_____

_____

_____

_____

_____

_____

_____

_____

_____

_____

_____

_____

_____

_____

_____

Questions

> "The future has great power over us. When it is filled with dread, we retreat into the past, but when it is filled with hope, we stride forward."
>
> **Richard Peace**

Where is God leading you?

_____

_____

_____

_____

How do you know?

_____

_____

_____

_____

List the scriptures, comments from others, and other signs supporting your direction.

_____

_____

_____

_____

What are you reading/watching?

_____

_____

_____

_____

What Bible/faith/spiritual growth studies or groups are you attending?

_____

_____

_____

_____

Have you thought about how much your favorite authors have struggled in order to express what you admire and enjoy in their writing? God reveals to each one of us individually. Are you relying only on someone else's answers?

_____

_____

_____

_____

Who have you been talking to?

_____

_____

_____

_____

Do you only seek advice from friends just like yourself? Find a verse about "wise counsel" in the Bible or your preferred book of faith and make a list of people who fit the description.

_____

_____

_____

_____

_____

_____

_____

You are a creative person. You can't help it because you are made in God's image and God is endlessly creative. God is at work in you right now. What is your faith community nurse/health ministry like in your imagination?

_____

_____

_____

_____

Dealing with Dragons

Name your dragons (fears/frustrations). Honestly tell yourself what fears are preventing you from moving toward your dreams and goals. Don't forget about **a fear that often paralyzes us just when we start to reach our goals: the fear of success.** Women often fear that they will pay dearly for their accomplishments. They frequently associate success with the loss of femininity and attractiveness, as well as the loss of relationships. To defeat this dragon, successful women need a strong support system.

In a perfect world, success is greeted with open arms. Unfortunately, in our world, failure is the accepted outcome. Have you ever had these thoughts?

- If I succeed, I will be expected to continue to succeed.
- It is easier not to try.
- It has been this way as long as I can remember.
- My life may not be what I want it to be, but it could get worse if I tried to change it.
- If I succeed, then I will have something in my life worth losing.
- My life is far from perfect, but at least I am in control of it.

God speaks in our surroundings, our health, our circumstances, in people around us, as well as in our intellect and that sometimes overactive thing we call a conscience. **Comprehension of the invisible begins with the visible.** Your journal is a place to examine the concrete things in your life. In doing so, you uncover things below the surface that have been hidden from your consciousness. You are able to see what was shadowed before. The hard part is acting when your idea and God's leading don't match. The choice is always yours.

> *"We should be taught not to wait for inspiration to start a thing. Action always generates inspiration. Inspiration seldom generates action."*
>
> **Frank Tibolt**

Reflect on this statement: "What I like to do most affords me all the opportunities I desire to live my life as God intended."

_____

_____

_____

_____

What is holding you back or pushing you forward?

_____

_____

_____

_____

_____

_____

_____

If you knew that you could not fail, what might your life and health ministry become with God's leading?

_____

_____

_____

_____

_____

_____

_____

_____

_____

_____

_____

_____

_____

_____

_____

_____

_____

_____

Journaling Tips

- Consider recording your dreams. Dreams can reveal what is going on inside your head and heart at a subconscious level.

- Look for patterns in your life. What is dying/declining in your life? (Relationships, commitments, career, dreams, goals) What is blooming? Where are signs of growth?

Day 5: So Much to Do — So Little Time

One of the most common complaints of faith community nurse/health ministry is the lack of time. Most likely, you already have that problem! What are you going to do about it? If you are miserable and constantly making the wrong decisions, if you are constantly running and have no time to be quiet before God, explore the possibility that on some unconscious level you are more comfortable with your misery than you are with the thought of change. *"Better the devil you know."*

Imagine that you have tried unsuccessfully all week to get caught up with everything you have to do, tried to keep everyone happy, and tried to be everything to everybody. Your body may be showing signs of stress overload like inability to sleep, poor concentration, bad mood, depression.

Time Assessment

Assess your time commitment. Determine if you are a good steward of your time. Keep track of your activities hourly for several days after you return home. Then add up the time spent for each category you have come up with.

> *"Every happening great and small is a parable whereby God speaks to us; And the art of life is to get the message."*
>
> **Malcolm Muggeridge**

Sample Categories:

Kids' sports	Travel	Service to Others
Schoolwork	Shopping	Church Activities
Sleeping	Reading	Housework
Eating	Exercise	Family Time
Work	Prayer	Journaling

My Categories:

_____	_____	_____
_____	_____	_____
_____	_____	_____
_____	_____	_____

Day 1

Day 2

Questions

What did you discover?

_____

_____

_____

_____

_____

Were there any surprises?

_____

_____

_____

_____

_____

Are you spending your time as you need to reach your goals?

_____

_____

_____

_____

_____

How do you find balance between work, play, and worship?

_____

_____

_____

_____

_____

_____

How are you wasting time?

_____

_____

_____

_____

_____

_____

What do you need to change?

_____

_____

_____

_____

_____

_____

Effective time stewards include time for recreation and reflection to avoid burnout. Remember schedules are only tools, keep them flexible. Think back to the goals you have written about in your journal. If you truly want to reach those goals, you must commit time to them. The more you plan your own time, the less you will have your time stolen by other people and unimportant events.

Reflect on ways you have used your time well.

_____

_____

_____

_____

_____

_____

_____

_____

Use this space as a "**recycle bin**" to write about the time consumers that you could get rid of in order to make room for what you really want to do with your time. This could include meetings, activities, social events, TV, relationships and possessions. Unfortunately, GOOD often gets in the way of BEST.

_____

_____

_____

_____

_____

_____

Create a new schedule for tomorrow with what you find important in it.

_____

_____

_____

_____

_____

_____

_____

Do you only seek advice from friends just like yourself? Find a verse about "wise counsel" in the Bible or your preferred book of faith and make a list of people who fit the description.

_____

_____

_____

_____

_____

_____

_____

You are a creative person. You can't help it because you are made in God's image and God is endlessly creative. God is at work in you right now. What is your faith community nurse/health ministry like in your imagination?

_____

_____

_____

_____

_____

_____

_____

_____

Journaling Tips

- Schedule time to write and private time with God as if it were a doctor's appointment.

- Open your journal with a prayer, a hymn or song, a quote, picture, or anything else that speaks to you and helps you to focus.

- Journals are aids for other spiritual practices such as:

  - **Bible study and other spiritual growth texts**—Take notes on a verse or paragraph and your understanding of it.

  - **Prayer**—Keep track of your prayers, who you are praying for, what you are praying for, and results. Copy prayers that speak to you as you learn to pray.

  - **Meditation**—Reflect on your life, experiences, books, music, movies, and quotes.

  - **Confession** – Don't forget the forgiveness!

Day 6: Where Do You Go From Here?

You have traveled through many topics in your journal. You started with activities to become acquainted with yourself. You explored why you exist in this place at this particular time. You have written personal mission statements and looked at goals and things you want to do before you die. Then you focused on your spiritual journeys and how God might reveal Himself and His plans for you. You have looked into shadows and named monsters on this journey.

Spiritual disciplines are not meant to be practiced entirely in isolation. We all need encouragement and understanding. We also need to learn from and be accountable to each other. We need a safe group to share fear, anger, and frustration, along with joy, love, and success.

Who can you count on for support and encouragement?

_____

_____

_____

_____

_____

_____

3 John 1-2

Beloved, I wish above all things that thou mayest prosper and be in health, even as thy soul prospereth.

What have you learned from your spiritual journaling experience?

_____

_____

_____

_____

_____

Journaling Tips

- Learn more about journaling by taking a class.

- Read articles by James Pennebaker and Kathleen Adams, two of the leading experts in journal-writing.

Resources

- International Parish Nurse Resource Center - www.churchhealthcenter.org/fcnhome
- Church Health Center - www.churchhealthcenter.org
- Health Ministries Association - www.HMAssoc.org
- Canadian Association for Parish Nurse Ministry - www.capnm.ca
- Nurses Christian Fellowship - www.ncf.org
- Journal of Christian Nursing - http://journals.lww.com/journalofchristiannursing/pages/default.aspx
- Sharon T. Hinton's website - www.sharonthinton.com

Dr. Sharon T. Hinton DMIN, RN-BC, MSN

Sharon is a faith community nurse health ministry educator and consultant for the International Parish Nurse Resource Center, a division of the Church Health Center in Memphis, Tennessee, the Executive Director of Rural Nurse Resource, Inc, and certified as a faith community nurse by the American Nurses Credentialing Center.

Sharon is a member of the Sigma Theta Tau International Honor Society of Nursing Speakers Bureau and speaks nationally about many topics including faith community nursing, health ministry and spiritual journaling for personal and professional growth.

She is the author of the "Nurse in the Church" column for the <u>Journal of Christian Nursing</u> and <u>the Spiritual Reflections Journal for Nurses and Health Advocates</u> along with many other articles, devotions, and continuing education materials as well as stories for <u>Chicken Soup for the Nurses Soul: Second Dose</u> and <u>Chicken Soup for the Soul: Food & Love</u>.

Sharon began her nursing career as a diploma graduate of the East Tennessee Baptist Hospital School of Nursing. She completed a Bachelors of Science in Nursing Degree at Texas Tech University School of Nursing and a Master of Science Degree in Parish Nursing as well as a Masters Certificate in Pastoral Studies at Saint Joseph's College of Maine. Sharon has a Doctor of Ministry degree in Global Health and Wholeness from Saint Paul's School of Theology in Kansas City. She is currently completing studies in spiritual direction and is a member of Spiritual Directors International.

She lives on the family farm in rural West Texas with a menagerie of cows, pets, and wildlife.

Contact Information:

Sharon@sharonthinton.com

www.sharonThinton.com

Rural Nurse Resource, Inc.
312 West Georgia Street
Floydada, TX 79235
(806)983-8096